The Little
Black Book of
Chat-up Lines
and Flirting

THE LITTLE BLACK BOOK OF CHAT-UP LINES AND FLIRTING

Summersdale Publishers Ltd
46 West Street
Chichester
West Sussex
PO19 1RP
UK

www.summersdale.com

Printed and bound in Czech Republic

ISBN: 978-1-84953-194-8

Substantial discounts on bulk quantities of Summersdale books are available to corporations, professional associations and other organisations. For details contact Summersdale Publishers by telephone: +44 (0) 1243 771107, fax: +44 (0) 1243 786300 or email: nicky@summersdale.com.

The Little Black Book of Chat-up Lines and Flirting

Jake Harris

CONTENTS

INTRODUCTION

Twenty-ton penguin!
Well, I had to break the ice somehow...

'Can I buy you a drink?' All very well if you're into the whole brevity thing. 'What's your sign?' Could get you into a seriously boring conversation. If you've ever been surrounded by hotties and stuck for an opening line, this cheeky little guide to getting started with the opposite sex will ensure you never miss an opportunity again.

To be young, free and single has its benefits, but if you're reading this book, then you've already decided to risk giving up all that – whether temporarily or permanently – for some action or at least interaction with the fairer sex. You can worry about who hogs the duvet and leaving the toilet seat down later on.

Oh, sorry, you're after a quick shag? Well, you may want to skip ahead to the more direct approach later in this book...

THE ART OF THE OPENER

A chat-up line is simply intended to show that you are attracted to a person in some way and to get their attention. Often the line itself is incidental to starting the conversation. The good thing about the subtle approach is you're not actually chatting her up, you're just talking, right? And if up close you realise she's not the hottie you thought, you're safe to escape...

CONVERSATION OPENERS

A chat-up line that falls flat can leave you red-faced with embarrassment. If someone thinks they're being chatted up, chances are they may put up barriers. You may have more success if you start by asking a question. A non-threatening question may lead to a conversation.

If you can ask about something she's reading or wearing without overstepping the bounds of politeness, so much the better. Or you could try opening with a piece of trivia... Read the paper and pick out one fact that you find interesting, and use it to open a discussion.

'I think there's something wrong with my phone. Could you try calling it for me to see if it rings?'

'Know what's the best thing about being single? Being able to talk to you.'

'Excuse me, are you accepting applications for your fan club because I'd like to join.'

'Nice to meet you, I'm [name]
and you are... gorgeous!'

'I have a pen and you have
a phone number... think
of the possibilities!'

'I would guess you're
against hunting – am I right?
Because you're a fox!'

'You're so beautiful that you've probably heard every chat-up line in the book.'

'Let me introduce myself – I'm your future husband.'

'I have had a really bad day and it always makes me feel better to see a pretty girl smile. So, would you smile for me?'

'I'm going to get in touch with the Ordnance Survey people to let them know I've found an area of outstanding natural beauty.'

'What's a lovely person like you doing around people like me?'

PLAYING THE GAME

Don't use that old excuse about saving yourself for the right woman. How will you know if you're not out there meeting them? When you find her, you want to make sure you know how to reel her in, so there's no time like the present to start working on your schmoozing style. Most people admire a bit of confidence and the ability to go up and talk to people will get you a long way.

GSOH

Making someone laugh is half the battle – everyone knows that a good sense of humour is high up on a woman's wish list. Generally women find witty men very attractive, and using a funny chat-up line also shows confidence, another characteristic women like in a man. If you can make a woman laugh, then you are definitely onto a winner! Just make sure you perfect the art of telling them...

GIFT OF THE GAB

Approaching a member of the opposite sex – a complete stranger – is a tough thing to do. Even if you are the very embodiment of charm and have looks that could kill (or at least maim!) at ten paces, if you can't make a person feel comfortable talking to you then the chances are it won't lead to seeing them again. You need to get talking. If the person likes you, they'll want to keep the conversation going anyway – it's just knowing where to start.

'Are you from Tennessee?
Cos you're the only
ten I see!'

'Is this the Starship
Enterprise? Because you
are out of this world!'

'You must be Jamaican...
because Jamaican me horny!'

'Do you have any raisins?
How about a date then?'

[shaking your watch]: 'I've got this
brilliant new watch with a special
sensory device that tells me you're
not wearing any underwear!'
[she says]: 'Nice try, I am
wearing underwear.'
[respond]: 'Ah, I must re-set it —
it's obviously an hour or so fast.'

'If you had a ladder in your
tights, it would be called a
stairway to heaven.'

'Sorry to bother you but I suffer from amnesia. Do I come here often?'

'I know I'm not the best-looking bloke here, but beauty is only a light switch away.'

'Your eyes are the same colour as my Porsche. And yes, they're both things I've only seen in my dreams.'

'My friend thinks you're beautiful, and if it's any consolation so do I.'

'Hi, I'm a postman, so you can rely on me to deliver a large package.'

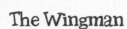

The Wingman

It sounds like strategy but women often enjoy the witty banter of two men, which can seem less aggressive and awkward than the targeted approach of one. Bring along a mate (preferably an ugly one!) to get the conversation started, but make sure she realises he's the clown and you're the sensitive one.

A TOUCH
OF CLASS

Most people like to be made a fuss of, and while being upfront can work for some conquests, it might also pay to show a little sophistication and hit your target with something that will stimulate their mind as well as their nether regions. Flattering someone with witty lines and romantic gestures shows that you could be a keeper.

THE OLD-FASHIONED ROMANTIC

You're a modern guy, you want to find
yourself a modern girl... naturally you are
going to look to the latest technology
to help you find, and hopefully keep,
the perfect partner. But don't overlook
the benefits of old-fashioned romantic
traditions – they've been wooing girls
successfully for centuries. Cook her a
candlelit dinner, make her a 'mixtape' (the
proper way – yes, that means recording
her favourite songs onto a CD, not giving
her an iTunes voucher), write a poem or
love letter, or turn up on her doorstep
with flowers and chocolates – they may be
clichéd but you can rest assured she won't
be turning any of these things down!

Love is a temporary madness.

Louis de Bernières

The only true gift is a portion of yourself.

Ralph Waldo Emerson

The course of true love never did run smooth.

William Shakespeare

Love is composed of a single soul inhabiting two bodies.

Aristotle

Who ever loved, that loved not at first sight?

Christopher Marlowe

There is no instinct like that of the heart.

Lord Byron

There is only one happiness in life: to love and be loved.

George Sand

Never close your lips to those whom you have already opened your heart.

Charles Dickens

*Kisses are a better
fate than wisdom.*

e. e. cummings

Love is the only gold.

Alfred Lord Tennyson

*Love is most nearly itself when
here and now cease to matter.*

T. S. Eliot

AL FRESCO LOVIN'

What could possibly be more romantic than surprising your date with a picnic in a local beauty spot, complete with champagne and strawberries? Remember to take an umbrella in case it rains – unless you want to go the whole hog and engage in some passionate movie-style kissing in the rain, in which case you can leave it at home.

SPEED
SEDUCTION

**Someone once wrote that men are
sexual bulldozers, while women are
sexual window boxes, and if you try to
tend a window box with a bulldozer...
There again – well, sometimes the
more direct approach is worth a try.**

Successful Speed Dating

From its humble beginnings in California in 1999, speed dating has become one of the most popular ways to find a potential partner. Be natural – you want to appear interested (and interesting), but don't lay it on with a trowel and declare your undying love – pay a compliment but make it one that is genuine, and don't act out of sorts in an attempt to be memorable.

'All those curves, and me with no brakes...'

'You must be a human light switch – every time I see you, you turn me on!'

'I always had trouble when I was a kid learning the alphabet. I still think U and I should be together.'

'Do you know the difference
between sex and conversation?
Want to talk about it?'

'Get your coat, you've pulled.'

'Sorry if I'm wrong, but
don't you want to kiss me?'

'Do you have to
have a special
licence for
that? For
driving me
crazy?'

'Do you sleep
on your
stomach?
Can I?'

'How would you like your
eggs in the morning?
Fertilised?'

'Is that a mirror in your
pocket? Because I can see
myself in your pants!'

'Let's get something
straight between us.'

SPEED DATING DOS AND DON'TS

DO pay attention to how you look – women aren't going to be impressed with a bloke in tracksuit bottoms and a beer-stained T-shirt.

DON'T waste valuable seconds asking boring questions. People speed date for the excitement of a flash-meeting with interesting people, so convince the girl that you could be the super-cool and interesting love of their life by knocking them out with a stonker like, 'What's your biggest unfulfilled ambition?' or 'Tell me about one of your passions'.

DO make an effort to smile and talk to people during breaks – they are all in the same boat as you!

DON'T get stuck with one of your definite 'nos' after the event – excuse yourself politely but firmly so that you can move on to more intriguing prospects.

CLASSIC ROMANTIC

Romance and compliments are still important, perhaps more than ever, and many women will give you credit for being romantic, as long as you are honest. Try to say something specific about her appearance – but if one of these lines can make her laugh first, so much the better...

MANNERS FROM A HUNDRED YEARS AGO THAT SOMETIMES HOLD TRUE TODAY:

Court Scientifically:

If you court at all, court scientifically. Bungle whatever else you will, but *do not bungle courtship.*

Speak Correctly:

Remember that all 'slang' is vulgar. It has become of late unfortunately prevalent, and we have known even ladies pride themselves on the saucy chique with which they adopt certain cant phrases of the day. *A gentleman should never permit any phrase that approaches to an oath, to escape his lips in the presence of a lady.*

Up and At It:

Dress up, spruce up, and be on the alert. Don't wait too long to get one much more perfect than you are; but *settle on some one soon*.

The Rejected Partner:

If a lady should civilly decline to dance with you, making an excuse, and you chance to see her dancing afterwards, do not take any notice of it, nor be offended with her. It might not be that she despised you, but that she preferred another. *We cannot always fathom the hidden springs which influence a woman's actions*.

'They say everything's made in China these days. Good to see some things are still made in heaven.'

'Ow! Sorry about the limp. I hurt my knee, falling for you.'

'You remind me of a parking ticket. You've got "fine" written all over you.'

'Is your surname Jacobs?
Because, girl,
you're a cracker.'

'Is that a fox on your shoulder,
or am I seeing double?'

'Did the sun come out or
did you just smile at me?'

'Is your father a thief? Because someone stole the stars from the sky and put them in your eyes.'

'I'm thinking of calling the police, because you stole my heart from across the room.'

'Your lips look so sweet –
I swear I could give up sugar
for life if I kissed you!'

'Is it hot in here,
or is it just you?'

'Do you believe in love at
first sight, or should I
walk past you again?'

Did You Know...?

- Medical experts say you're more likely to catch the common cold by shaking hands than by kissing.

- There are more than 900 varieties of red roses.

- The oldest sex manuals were produced in China 5,000 years ago.

GOLDEN OLDIES

Sure, these lines have been used a million times before, but never in precisely this context so go for it if you want to get the message across loud and clear...

'Tell me, what's it really
like in heaven? Because
you must be an angel...'

'Apart from being sexy,
what do you do for a living?'

'Were you in the Guides?
Because you sure have tied
a good knot in my heart.'

'Sorry for staring at you – I just want to remember your face for my dreams.'

'When God made you, he was showing off.'

'There must be something
wrong with my eyes; I
can't take them off you.'

'Are your legs tired? You've
been running through my
mind ever since I saw you!'

'I think the police are looking
for you... It's got to be
illegal to look that good.'

'Your eyes are blue like the ocean and I'm lost at sea.'

'You look like my first wife. Seriously. My friends are always asking me when I'm going to get married.'

'Excuse me, I'm new around here. Could you give me directions to your bedroom?'

Just One Look

Women enjoy being admired and one of the sexiest things you can do is simply look. A flattering glance of admiration will make a woman feel special and will give her pleasure, something she will remember. Sometimes it's best not to say anything right away. Keep her guessing for a while.

THE
PERFECT TEN

That one person may bring you out in a
cold sweat but, unfortunately, there's
no such thing as the perfect ten chat-up
lines! But put on a sparkling smile and
your most devilish charm, take a deep
breath and give it a try...

'Can I have a picture of you so I can show Santa what I want for Christmas?'

'You're so hot, you're making me melt.'

'Is there a rainbow? You look like the treasure I've been searching for...'

'Pick a number between one
and ten. Sorry, wrong!
You'll have to take off
all your clothes.'

'Do you work with
the airlines? Because my
heart is taking off.'

'I hope you know first aid,
'cause you take my
breath away.'

'Hurry up! My lips won't kiss themselves.'

'Life is a big jigsaw puzzle – and you are the missing piece.'

'You looked bored so I
thought I'd cheer you up...
I thought my face might
make you laugh.'

'Smile! It's the second
best thing you can do
with your lips...'

SIX THINGS THAT YOU MAKE YOU MORE ATTRACTIVE

1. Work out just enough to give yourself muscle tone and better skin tone.
2. Be upbeat and positive.
3. Communicate.
4. Listen.
5. Show that you're good fun to be with.
6. Offer her a foot massage.

KILLER PUT-DOWNS

Ouch! Nobody likes to be turned down. Maybe she just doesn't fancy you, or she really is just having fun with her mates, or has a boyfriend. But maybe it's just a bit of banter, so be ready for a comeback yourself! Forewarned is forearmed...

'Shall we go all the way?'
'Sure – you go all the way
to your place and I'll go
all the way to mine.'

'I'd love to get into
your knickers.'
'There's already one arsehole in
there, and that's plenty,
thank you.'

'Where have you been
all my life?'
*'I wasn't even born for
the first half of it.'*

'Let's be honest, we've both
come here for the same reason.'
*'You're right. I wanted to
meet someone attractive and
interesting. I just haven't seen
anyone yet.'*

[Call her over using your finger]

'I made you come using just one finger. Imagine what I could do with my whole hand!'

'Would it be fair to say you're a complete wanker?'

'When I was a prisoner of war
they tortured me on the rack,
and it wasn't just my
legs they stretched...'
*'Clearly they also stretched
your imagination.'*

'You bring me out
in a hot sweat.'
*'You bring me out
in an allergic rash.'*

'I could get lost in your eyes.'
'Why don't you just get lost?'

'You know what you'd
look great in? My bed.'
*'I would offer to shag your
brains out, but someone's
clearly beaten me to it.'*

'Are you free
tomorrow
night?'
'No, and
you couldn't
afford me.'

LOCATION, LOCATION, LOCATION

A sterling chat-up line isn't going to get you anywhere if the only place you're using it is in front of your bedroom mirror. Knowing where to find the kind of girl you're after is key, so if you're after someone in particular, take some time to consider a likely location. If you're not that fussy, why not try some of these...

TEN PLACES TO MEET WOMEN

1. **Salsa dance class:** women love to dance and very often there aren't enough male partners to go round at classes.

2. **Outdoor activities and events:** whether you're getting physical or it's theatre or a concert, being outdoors can be a lot less threatening than a 'meat market' nightclub.

3. **Language class:** remember how sexy a foreign language can sound, and women like men who are interested in the world.

4. **Art gallery cafe:** you don't need to know anything about art to show an interest, and women are much more intrigued by the idea of meeting men in romantic and unusual settings.

5. **Public transport:** if there's someone you see every day and she makes eye contact, find a subtle way to get a little closer and start a conversation.

6. **Volunteering:** if a man is already showing that he thinks about others, it sends the message that he will care about the woman in his life.

7. **Shopping:** it stands to reason that the more you go shopping, the more women you'll meet; food shopping is ideal...

8. **Wine tasting:** it's something different and you never know, she may find it as ridiculous as you do...

9. **Walking the dog:** it doesn't have to be your dog, but make sure you borrow a cute one.

10. Singles holidays: you're away from home, you're with single women – what's not to like?

BODY TALK

It's not just what comes out of your mouth that can score points with the opposite sex – aside from the messages your general appearance can give off, there are certain subliminal signals that are given off by your movements and position which can indicate whether you're striking the right chord or not...

IS SHE INTERESTED?

No body language is a sure way of 'reading' someone, but it's worth paying attention, especially if there's a combination of signs:

Playing with her hair – **touching it unconsciously shows she's at ease in your company.**

Being careful about the way she eats or drinks or puts on lipstick – **shows she cares about how she looks.**

Adjusting her clothes to make sure they look good – **she wants to look her best.**

Looking at you and smiling – **it sounds obvious but if she's not, there may be something wrong.**

Unintentionally mirroring your actions – **there may be a connection happening between you.**

BODY LANGUAGE

The forearm is packed with pleasure nerves that respond best to a touch travelling one to ten centimetres per second, according to a scientific report in medical journal *Nature Neuroscience.* These 'C-tactile' nerve fibres send signals to the limbic system, an area of the brain associated with trust and affection. So touching or stroking someone's forearm could be just the right move to cross the 'touch barrier'.

DUTCH COURAGE

If you're in a bar or a pub and you've
already made eye contact, you're halfway
there. Take a deep breath, don't forget
to smile, and play the game... Easier said
than done. How come your mates couldn't
shut you up a minute ago, and now your
mouth's gone all dry? Maybe just one
more pint of Courage is needed. Just don't
leave it until so late in the evening that
you're babbling incoherently. You might
get her phone number – but will you be
able to read it in the morning?

Pucker Up

Women are far more likely to want to have sex with you if you're a good kisser. With a first kiss, less is more: don't smother her with saliva and choke her with too much tongue. Start gently, initiate the first move and make sure your breath is fresh.

ELECTRIC LADYLAND

Some might say that there's nothing like the real thing, but nowadays flirting doesn't have to be done face-to-face – hopeful romantics can connect via the Internet using instant messaging and online dating sites, as well as by texting. Essentially the rules are the same, though you need to be ready when it comes to taking it from cyberspace to real-world interaction.

KEEP IT REAL

It's so much easier to type out your feelings from the safety of your desk or from a distance on your mobile than it is to express them in a real-life conversation, and it pays to be aware of this and think about exactly what message you are putting across. Does a kiss at the end of a text or email always mean flirting is taking place? Perhaps not – but if you're getting mixed signals the best thing you can do is ask – at least she won't see your face turning red if you've got the wrong end of the stick!

SAUCY SMILEYS

The Wink ;)
Cheeky, cheerful and bound to lighten the mood.

The Eyelash Bat ;;)
You're feeling flirty (or you've got something in your eye!).

The Kiss :*
More than your average 'x'.

The Bunny

```
 (\ /)
( Y )
(   )
C(")(")
```

Lovestruck :X
For laying it on thick.

The Angel 0:)
Flattery of the supernatural kind.

The Devil >:)
For when you're feeling naughty.

The Hug >:D<
For when you're feeling lovey dovey.

The Blush :">
For when you want to play coy.

The Heart ♥
For a romantic touch.

The Rose

@)};----

The Tongue :P

Good for being cheeky and for licking.

MAKING A DATE

Most people will eventually want their online romance to blossom into a real-life relationship and there's no reason why this shouldn't be successful. However, remember that appearances can be deceptive – at worst the person could be straight-up lying about themselves or you may find that they're actually even more likeable in person than they are on screen – either way, expect your feelings to be tested when you meet face-to-face.

HOW TO INTERPRET AN INTERNET DATING PROFILE PHOTO:

No Photo:
Looks-wise, I'm more *National Geographic* than *Nuts*.

Oddly Positioned Webcam Photo:
I spend at least five hours a day trawling dating websites, in between updating my Facebook page.

Revealing Torso Shot:
Don't forget your toothbrush.

Tattoos and Piercings Galore:
Don't forget the TCP.

Chirpy Portrait Shot:
I'm an agreeable and largely normal person (as far as my photo goes).

HOLLYWOOD STYLE

Lots of women are suckers for a good Hollywood rom-com ending – the type of climax to a film that involves revelations, rain, tears, kissing and loud dramatic music. If you're getting somewhere but you haven't quite sealed the deal, why not go all-out and try an overblown gesture as seen on the silver screen?

Draw her portrait á la *Titanic:*

if you can get her in the nude then chances are you've already done the hard work!

Serenade her from outside her window:

yes, it's been done to death, but it beats climbing a drainpipe and you're less likely to end up in A & E.

Share a plate of meatballs and offer her the last one:
a cheaper alternative is to offer her your last Rolo.

A bunch of flowers?
How about a bunch of *flours*?

Look Like a Leading Man

Women fork out nearly £500m a year on cosmetics for their other halves, which works out as one of the most expensive hints in history. The fairer sex don't want to be accosted by smelly, unkempt men who haven't shaved for five days and look like they've spent the night in a dustbin. Make time to groom and your potential targets may appreciate you that little bit more.

GETTING PHYSICAL

The devil makes work for idle hands, so why not put yours to good use and get touchy-feely when you're flirting? Physical contact while chatting someone up can be potent – a gentle hand on an elbow while you're delivering a line has an immediate impact and can really help to get the message across. On the other hand you might find success with a more fun approach by making a game of it – just make sure it's done with a twinkle in your eye, backed up with a witty line (rather than simply going for a good old grope!).

PALM READING

Palm reading is an ancient art, but it can work just as well in the context of flirting. Asking if you can read a girl's palm gives you the opportunity to take her hand in yours and run your fingers over her skin. It also gives you the chance to flatter her by saying the lines indicate a 'passionate person, bursting with sexual energy'.

EYEBALL READING

Before going for this one, make sure your breath is minty-fresh. To perform an eyeball reading you need to stand nose to nose, staring directly into each other's eyes. Pretend to 'read' the lines of the iris, explaining that the person's perfect match can be determined by the patterns in their eyes – since you're doing the reading you can simply describe yourself!

MASSAGE

It may be an oldie, but it's a goodie.
To be fully prepared, learn some basic
techniques of neck and back massage
before diving in and squishing the life
out of someone. If a girl mentions they
have back or neck pain, it's an ideal
opportunity to get busy with your hands,
or you could simply mention that
you love giving massages.

DOWN AND DIRTY

Let's face it – lots of girls go for the bad boy. Sometimes this means you have to play it cool and sometimes it means you can go all out and be downright dirty. If you get the right girl, being cheeky and a little bit smutty can be a big winner, and a fast-track to getting jiggy with it in the bedroom. 'Many a true word is said in jest' as they say, so when you're being rude in a fun way you are also giving off the signal that you're serious about getting physical. Here are a few lines that are naughty but nice.

'Do you want to play army?
I will "lay down" and you
can blow the hell out of me.'

'I've just received government
funding for a four-hour
expedition to find your G-spot.'

'There are 256 bones
in your body. Would
you like another?'

'If you were a lolly, I would be licking you all night!'

'I own the best roller coaster in town – would you like to ride it?'

'Want to play TV? I'll play with your knobs while you watch my antenna rise.'

'Nice shoes. Wanna screw?'

'Do you have a boyfriend?' ['Yes.'] 'Do you mess around?' ['No.'] 'Would you hold still while I do?'

'Hi, I've been undressing
you with my eyes all
night long and think it's
time to see if I'm right.'

'I suppose a shag's out
of the question?'

'I'll show you mine if
you show me yours.'

CRINGE-WORTHY GEMS

Making an arse of yourself by using a truly heinous chat-up line is one way to break down the barriers and get a conversation going. However before you unleash one of these howlers make an assessment of her character – for instance, if she seems like the bookish type and the line bombs you can pretend you were being ironic and launch into a conversation about sexual dynamics in postmodern society.

'I'm a meteorologist and
I'd like to study your
warm front.'

'Hello, you don't know me but
I've just come back from the
future in which you and me have
the most passionate love affair.
And it started tonight, actually.'

'The best thing about you
would have to be my arms.'

'If I said you had a beautiful body would you hold it against me?'

'Do you have a map? I keep getting lost in your eyes.'

'There's something on
your face, I think
it's beauty...'

'You know, being a millionaire
can be pretty lonely without
someone to share it with.'

'If kisses were snowflakes
I'd send you a blizzard.'

'Did you just fart? Well
you blew me away.'

'You're so hot, I bet you're the
main cause of global warming!'

'Congratulations! You've won
first prize in a competition:
a date with me!'

THE
GREAT ESCAPE

If you like to engage in a little wordplay, regardless of the eventual outcome of the situation, then arm yourself with these put-downs to escape unwanted admirers.

'What's your idea of
a perfect evening?'
*The one I was having
before you came over.'*

'You've got the face of an angel.'
*'And you've got the face of a
Saint. A St Bernard.'*

'I've come from another planet
to seek out beautiful life forms.'
*'Is that because your
race is so ugly?'*

'I never forget a face.'
*'Neither do I, but in your case
I'll make an exception.'*

'When can we be alone?'
'When we're not with each other.'

'May I introduce myself?'
'Certainly – try those
people over there.'

'Can I flirt with you?'
'I was hoping to meet someone
younger – people might think
your my dad.'

'I think I could make
you very happy.'
'Why, are you leaving?'

'How did you get
to be so beautiful?'
'I must have got your share.'

'I'm sure I've noticed you before.'
'That's funny, I haven't noticed you yet.'

AND FINALLY...
JUST FOR LAUGHS

**Cheesy lines are high-risk but
at least they are cheeky, and
laughter is better than silence!**

'You're hot, I'm cool. Maybe
if we got together we
could even things out.'

'Do you know what winks
and shags like a tiger?'
['No.'] [Wink.]

'Fuck me if I'm wrong,
but isn't your name Hilda?
['No.'] 'Well then, I guess
you'll just have to...'

'Is your last name Gillete
because you look like
the best a man can get.'

'Do you know the difference
between a hamburger and
a blow job? No? Let's have
lunch sometime...'

'Do you have a boyfriend?
Well, when you want a MAN-
friend, come and talk to me!'

'You don't know me, but I dreamt about you last night and thought it only fair to introduce myself.'

'There's something wrong with my phone. Your number's not in it!'

'Want to see my scar?
My circumcision scar.'

'Did you just look at my bum?'
['No.'] 'Oh, that's a shame...'

'I'm like a Rubik's Cube.
The more you play with
me, the harder I get!'

'Do you believe in the
hereafter? Well, then I
guess you know what
I'm here after?'

'My name's [name], but you
can call me anytime.'

'Would you sleep with
a stranger?'
['No.'] 'Then let me introduce
myself properly...'

'I'd love to cook you dinner
sometime, on one condition...
You cook me breakfast.'

'Want to make babies?'
['No!'] 'Want to practise...?'

'What has 148 teeth and holds
back the Incredible Hulk?
The zip on my trousers!'

'You must be a general,
cos my privates just
stood up to attention.'

'I'll be the six,
if you'll be the nine.'

'What's a nice girl like
you doing in a dirty
mind like mine?'

There again, you could just try:

'Sorry, I know this is a bit forward, but if I don't ask you I might not see you again — could I call you sometime?'

www.summersdale.com